T0029051

FLASHBACK TO THE...
CHILL 2000s!

By Gloria Cruz
Illustrated by Sarah Rebar

Ready-to-Read

SIMON SPOTLIGHT
An imprint of Simon & Schuster's Children's Publishing Division
New York London Toronto Sydney New Delhi
1230 Avenue of the Americas, New York, New York 10020
This Simon Spotlight edition August 2023
Text copyright © 2023 by Simon & Schuster, Inc.
Illustrations copyright © 2023 by Sarah Rebar • Stock photos by iStock
All rights reserved, including the right of reproduction in whole or in part in any form.
SIMON SPOTLIGHT, READY-TO-READ, and colophon are registered trademarks of Simon & Schuster, Inc.
For information about special discounts for bulk purchases, please contact Simon & Schuster Special Sales at 1-866-506-1949
or business@simonandschuster.com.
Manufactured in the United States of America 0723 LAK
2 4 6 8 10 9 7 5 3 1
Cataloging-in-Publication Data is available from the Library of Congress.
ISBN 9781665940894 (pbk)
ISBN 9781665940900 (hc)
ISBN 9781665940917 (ebook)

GLOSSARY

BlackBerry: A wireless handheld device that allowed users to make phone calls, send emails, and access the Internet

Bling: A word used to describe shiny jewelry

Chillax: A combination of the words "relax" and "chill"

Da bomb: A term used to describe something very cool or awesome

DVD (digital video disc): A disc used to store data like movies and music

Fetch: A word that means "very fashionable"

Heelys: A brand of shoe that features a detachable wheel at the bottom of the heel and can also be used as roller skates

Poppin': A word meaning "cool"

Stoked: Another word for "excited"

Uggs: A style of furry sheepskin boots

Y2K: An acronym for the Year 2000

Note to readers: Some of these words may have more than one definition. The definitions above match how these words are used in this book.

CONTENTS

Chapter 1
Totally Rad Trends!

Are you ready
to take a trip back in time?
Lean back and enjoy the chill 2000s!

Put on your favorite pair of **Uggs**
as you learn about the **poppin'**
trends and fads that totally
ruled this decade.

The 2000s had cool toys, like
Furbies, Skip-Its, and Sillybandz,
and popular dolls, like
Bratz and My Scene.

Kids were also **stoked** about
the Nintendo Wii gaming system—
you'd dance in front of your
TV pretending to be a rock star
with games like *Just Dance*,
Rock Band, and *Guitar Hero*!

The Nintendo Wii is Nintendo's
most successful home console
ever, selling over 100 million
units worldwide by 2013!

Music technology in the 2000s was **da bomb.**
A device called the iPod was released. It could hold up to a thousand of your favorite songs and even some games!

The iPod Mini was released in 2004, making music even easier to bring on the go!

Music in the 2000s was off the hook! Pop, hip-hop, and country music were some of the most popular musical styles of the decade.

American Idol premiered in 2002, becoming one of the biggest singing competition shows of all time!

Flat-screen TVs became popular, and VHS tapes were being replaced with **DVDs**. People would pick a movie they wanted to watch on Netflix's website and have the DVD mailed to them. (Then they would mail it back.)

Netflix launched its streaming service to consumers in 2007, making it the Netflix we're all familiar with today!

And with TV stations like Disney Channel, Nickelodeon, and Cartoon Network, everyone had a favorite cartoon! Maybe it was *Kim Possible*, *Dora the Explorer*, *Teen Titans*, or *The Powerpuff Girls*.

Popular TV commercials during the 2000s introduced new snacks and drinks being released in super-funky colors.

Heinz ketchup turned
purple and green,
and Pepsi turned blue!

Food trends in the 2000s were anything but **chillaxed**. Eating healthy and organic foods became totally **fetch**!

Annual sales of organic food hit $24 billion by 2009!

But no one could resist the delicious drinks from Starbucks. And you totally had to get extra whipped cream on your Frappuccino!

Chapter 2
Fetch Fashion and Fads

Fashion in the 2000s was epic.
In this decade the **bling**,
footwear, and clothing
trends made very bold statements!

Bling included jewelry
that spelled out your name.
And mood rings and best-friend
charm necklaces were
total must-haves.

If you weren't into jewelry,
then you were probably expressing
yourself through your hairstyle.

Popular hairstyles included
chunky highlights
and cornrow braids.
And some people preferred
spiky hair with lots of hair gel!

Fashion in the 2000s was some of the best yet. Besties couldn't resist wearing matching Juicy Couture sweat suits. Staying comfortable in soft **Uggs** or in baggy clothes was key.

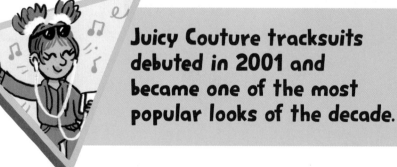

Juicy Couture tracksuits debuted in 2001 and became one of the most popular looks of the decade.

Or, you were probably walkin' by day and rollin' by night in your **Heelys**!

Other popular styles
and accessories included
oversized sunglasses,
mini purses,
tiny butterfly hair clips,
and trucker hats.

They were some of *the* trademark accessories during the 2000s!

Chapter 3
Stay Connected!

Types of communication
were on a *whole* new level
with the rise of social media,
which hit its stride in the 2000s.

Websites and games like Myspace, Facebook, and Club Penguin made it possible for people to stay in touch through the Internet. And on a new site called YouTube, anyone could post fun videos of themselves.

Facebook was created in 2004 by a student at Harvard University as a way for all of the students to connect with one another.

Methods of communicating were also totally changing. Gadgets like the **BlackBerry**, the Sidekick, and the iBook made the 2000s a decade to remember!

But one of the most iconic tech
inventions of the 2000s was the iPhone.
It was an iPod and touchscreen
cell phone in one!

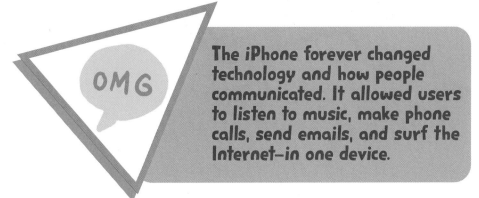

The iPhone forever changed
technology and how people
communicated. It allowed users
to listen to music, make phone
calls, send emails, and surf the
Internet—in one device.

And who could forget the rumors about **Y2K**? Since the types of computers we use today were invented in the 1900s, they were programmed to only show two digits instead of four for the year.

Everyone panicked, thinking that when
the calendar hit January 1, 2000,
(at the turn of the century),
computers would go to "00" and all
systems would think it was 1900!
This was called the "millennium bug."

To solve this problem,
the government stepped in,
instructing the computer
industry to use four digits for
years instead of two digits.

Wasn't that time-traveling adventure all that and a bag of chips?

The 2000s started a lot of the trends we see today. Well, it's time to bounce, so catch you next time!

2000s Throwbacks!

Here's a fun activity you and a grown-up can do together! Ask them if they have any items of clothing that could represent the looks from the 2000s. If they do, try to make some cool outfits of your own that you might have liked to wear if you had grown up in that decade.

Another fun activity you can do is look at old photos from the 2000s. Do you like any of the styles? Do you notice anything similar to what's popular today?